Anansi Traps a Snake

Cynthia Rider

Illustrated by Rhian Nest James

Oxford

"You can't get me, Anansi," said Snake.

"No," said Anansi. "You are too long."

"You are as long as this stick."

"Am I?" said Snake.

"Look!" said Anansi.

"Put your tail here."

"Put your head here."

"I am as long as the stick," said Snake.

"Yes," said Anansi. "You are very long."

"But you are not very smart!"

"I've got you now, Snake!"